MEMORY MAKERS

Punch *your* Art ~out~ 2

SATELLITE PRESS

PAM METZGER

Contents

KATHLEEN PANEITZ

This book is dedicated to paper and scrapbook artists who have discovered the magnificent wonders of punch art.
It is our hope that *Punch Your Art Out Volume 2* will be a source of creative inspiration for years to come.

KATHLEEN PANETZ

What is punch art?

Punch art is easy

All you need are a few punches and some paper to create captivating art from simple, punched paper shapes. Paper artists marvel at how rapidly punch art projects take on a life of their own, adding charm and whimsy to scrapbook pages, photo frames, cards, invitations and more. Punch art can also extend your scrapbooking budget by making good use of paper scraps that might otherwise be thrown away. Punch art offers versatility and endless possibilities.

Basic building blocks

Punches are the basic tools of punch craft. However, your choice of papers and use of a variety of tricks will add to the dimension and uniqueness of your art. Sources to help fuel your imagination include art books, posters, cards, fabrics, picture books, mail order catalogs and more.

Basic shapes and beyond

In punch art, as in life, all things consist of basic shapes. When basic shapes are combined, clever forms are created. Forms made from combined shapes surround us. In the example at right, you can see how hearts, a leaf, a circle, a star and a snowflake join together to become a whimsical robin. Look around you. Learning to "see in shapes" will enhance your ability to adapt real-life elements into punch art designs.

Themes

Photographs, fabrics, paper designs and artwork can influence the theme of your punched art. For example, a summer photo of family members splashing at the beach conjures up images of tropical fish, sand castles and seashells as shown on page 17. Likewise, an artist working on a holiday page may find inspiration from the fabric of her daughter's "Christmas bear" dress in a recent photo. By selecting design elements and colors that are customarily associated with your theme or subject, you're guaranteed to capture the sentiment that best complements your projects.

Start simple

Novice punch artists quickly learn that punch art is habit-forming, fulfilling and fun. Beginners shouldn't be intimidated by intricate designs or by possessing a small number of punches. Intricate designs are nothing more than basic combined elements, and you can always borrow punches, host a punching party or hand-cut designs when necessary. This book and its companion, *Punch Your Art Out Volume 1*, contain all the direction and inspiration you need to get started in the fascinating world of punch art. Start with simple designs, working your way up to more complex ones. Your passion for punch art will take flight while faith in your artistic abilities soars.

PAM KLASSEN

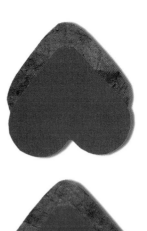

Hearts, birch leaf, star, snowflake and circle, when cut and combined, become a robin. Eyes are punched out with ⅛" round hand punch.

Introduction to punches

Tool up on punches

Today's punches come in a wide array of shapes, patterns and sizes. While punch sizes and names differ slightly among manufacturers, here are the most common types.

1 **Small Punch**
SCORPION SHOWN

2 **Medium Punch**
DAISY FLOWER #4 SHOWN

3 **Large/Jumbo Punch**
OLD TREE SHOWN

4 **Double & Mini Punches**
BUTTERFLY/OAK LEAF & FLOWER SHOWN

5 **Extension Punch**
HEART SHOWN
For reaching beyond the edges.

6 **Frame Punch**
STAR FRAME SHOWN

7 **Frame/Silhouette Punch**
SMILEY FACE DOUBLE FRAME SHOWN

8 **Corner Rounder Punch**
CORNER ROUNDER #CP-6 SHOWN

Punch care & trouble-shooting

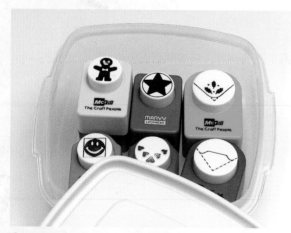

Storage

For years of service, store punches in a dry place to prevent rusting.

Sticky Punches

If paper keeps getting stuck in your punches, lubricate them as needed with lightweight sewing machine oil or WD-40®. Clean excess oil before punching paper. Or try punching through waxed paper a few times.

9 **Decorative Corner Punch**
HEARTS SHOWN
Creates corner patterns.

10 **Decorative Corner Rounder Punch**
HOLLY DECORATIVE CORNER ROUNDER SHOWN
Rounds and creates pattern at the same time.

11 **Corner Lace Only Punch**
CORNER LACE #47-LACE SHOWN

12 **Decorative Corner Lace Punch**
SCALLOP CORNER LACE EDGE SHOWN

13 **Corner Frame Punch**
CORNER FRAME #3261-00 SHOWN

13

15

16

12

9

11

10

14

14 **Border/Edge Punch**
HEARTS AND FLOWERS BORDER SHOWN

15 **Silhouette Punch**
GINGERBREAD MAN SILHOUETTE SHOWN

16 **Hand Punch**
¼" RECTANGLE HAND PUNCH SHOWN

17 **Six-in-one Punch**
6-IN-1 CHRISTMAS CRAFT PUNCH SHOWN

17

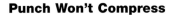

Punch Won't Compress

Make certain that the material you are punching through is not to thick. Use the palm of your hand and push down hard or place the punch on the floor and gently step on it. There are also a variety of punch compression aids on the market to make punching easier.

Sharpening Punches

When punches become dull, try punching through aluminum foil to sharpen. If necessary, punch through a very fine grade of sandpaper both right side up and upside down to sharpen all edges.

Suggested tools & supplies

- Pigment Pens/Markers
- Regular and Decorative Rulers
- Acid- and Lignin-Free Paper
- Regular and Decorative Scissors
- Craft Knife
- Tweezers
- Photographs
- Tissue and Wrapping Paper
- Postcards and Greeting Cards

Basic to advanced techniques

Layering

By combining and positioning different punched shapes, you can create an endless number of new images. Layering also adds dimension to punched designs–simply build layers of the same shape to create depth.

Snipping

Punched shapes can be redefined by snipping into the primary shape with a second punch or scissors, thus creating a whole new primary image.

Cutting

By cutting punched shapes you can combine paper colors and patterns for unique effects or remove extraneous portions of punched shapes.

Using negative pieces

Those little pieces left over after you have punched a silhouette, frame, or even border shape can be used for other punch designs. Layer and arrange them to add detail and dimension.

- Photo-Safe Adhesives, Tapes & Splits
- Glue Sticks, Glue Pens and Sticky Dots
- Self-Adhesive Foam Spacers
- Adhesive Application Machine

Punch positioning

Proper punch positioning ensures accuracy. Begin with a sheet of paper that is larger than your anticipated finished design. Punch the smallest shape first. Flip the larger punch over and position the punched paper into the larger punch shape, thus working from the inside out.

Offset punching

Punch initial shape, then flip the punch upside down and offset previously punched shape to create a new one.

Removing corner guides

To increase the versatility of a corner punch, remove the plastic guides as shown. Now you can use the corner punch to create entire borders. You may want to reinstall the guides at a later date, so label them and store in a safe place.

Adding dimension

Add depth by using contrasting paper shades, patterned paper, layering punched shapes and by curling or folding punched shapes around a toothpick, pencil, tweezers or paintbrush handle.

Punch guidelines

For borders, draw guidelines and dots on back of paper. Insert paper into an upside down punch to align. View the guides and align for accuracy. For borders using a hand punch, draw guidelines on the back side of your paper. Place dots where the center of the punch should be. Or, tape grid paper to border strip with removable tape, punching through both papers for accuracy.

Application of adhesives

Adhesive photo splits or tapes can be cut to any size to accommodate a punched shape. Passing paper through an adhesive application machine before punching also provides a quick and uniform way to adhere adhesive.

Placement using tweezers or craft knife

Use tweezers or the tip of a craft knife to pick up and place adhesive-backed punched shapes. These tools can also be used to lift off the plastic adhesive backing on your small punched shapes.

Pen stroking

Pen stroke stitching has become a perennial favorite for punch artists to accent a punched shape design. Simply use the pen of your choice to "stitch" or doodle around your punched shape or outline the shape to make it stand out.

Border punch pieces

Use the negative pieces from borders to create squiggles, dots and many other shapes.

Textured & printed paper

There are a myriad of papers to choose from for your punch art. The same shape or design can look very different just by changing the paper, color, pattern or texture.

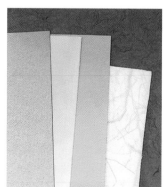

Combining shapes

Combining single punched shapes can enlarge and enhance a design. Four fleurs-de-lis combine to make a large flower; large flowers combine for an all-over pattern. Six medium snowflakes combine to make a large ring of snowflakes; the rings combine for an even larger pattern.

How paper choices can affect the outcome of your design

It's easy to take one simple design and completely change its appearance by changing the colors, patterns and textures of the papers used. For instance, note how the punched presents below change as the papers are changed.

A simple birthday design becomes…   a gorgeous Christmas design becomes…   an elegant wedding design!

Layering techniques

With a little imagination, a few punches can go a long way. The pansy at left is created by layering different shades of medium and small apples. The flower center is made up of three small hearts topped with three ⅛" rounds from a hand punch. This type of layering adds depth and dimension to punch designs.

summer florals & gardening

PAM KLASSEN

The long, hot days of summer are the perfect time to bring the outdoors inside with these cool summer punch art designs.

3-D Summer Lilacs
Butterflies & Blooms Page

LILACS—Small heart, diamond mini extension, negative squares from southwest border, ¹⁄₁₆" round hand punch. Cut small purple hearts in half; join four halves for each lilac flower. Glue diamond, square and ¹⁄₁₆" round hand-punched shapes in center. Make dozens of lilacs and set aside.

LILAC BUDS—Small heart. Roll one small purple heart around end of tweezers, dab tip with glue and fold small green heart over the end to hold bud together. Make dozens of buds, set aside.

LILAC LEAVES—Medium heart. Fold medium green hearts in half. Slightly roll each half over a pencil to curl the leaf's edge. Make about thirty leaves and set them aside.

LARGE FLOWER BUDS—Old tree, medium heart. Cut trunk from old tree. Roll top of tree around tip of tweezers, glue tip and fit inside of rolled medium green heart to hold together. Set aside.

LARGE FLOWERS—Old tree, medium apple, small heart, ¹⁄₈" round hand punch. For each petal, glue apple on top of old tree (with trunk removed); roll slightly around pencil to curl. Make five petals and glue into a circle. Add hearts and circles in center to complete design and set aside.

ASSEMBLY—For art on left page, cut dark purple paper into curved cone shapes as supports and cover with tiny lilac flowers, gluing into place. Add buds to tips and green leaves intermittently for a realistic effect. Assemble all elements by layering and gluing in place, using tiny pieces of bent cardstock to hold cones in place and create the 3-dimensional look that you see here. Add large blue flowers and buds to complete the design. To assemble the page above, follow these instructions, omitting the use of cones and cardstock to elevate elements.

BUTTERFLY—(above) Medium butterfly, negative pieces from hearts and tears border.

3-D Floral Design

JOANN COLLEDGE, PHOTO SUSANNE SPICKER

Hand-cut birdhouse, roof and post. Add small doves, ¼" round hand punch, and negative pieces from flower decorative corner. Trim both photos and mats with corner rounder.

SUNFLOWER–Medium daisy, small circle, negative pieces from bear frame punch. Layer two medium daisies, then two small circles as shown. Fold and join to sunflower stalks made with negative pieces from bear frame, large birch leaves and small maple leaves.

LARGE FLOWER–Silhouette flower, ¼" round hand punch, small maple leaf. Layer silhouette flowers then ¼" rounds. Fold and join with small maple leaf.

SMALL FLOWER–Small shell, flower hand punch. Layer and fold shells and flowers.

SUNFLOWER

LARGE FLOWER

SMALL FLOWER

Mikko was so proud of his catch of the day. He released the little chipmunk from his powerful jaws in order that he could receive his hard earned praise. To his surprise Mikkos' new furry striped toy disappeared.

Cats are so gullible!

Where did he go?

He is here somewhere.

Morgan found the little guy later that day, when he fell from a hanging flower basket. He recovered quickly after having the wind knocked out of him and scurried off cursing at Mikko all the way.

Hollyhock Accents
HEATHER MCWHORTER

PETALS–Medium and/or small hearts trimmed with deckle scissors. Five trimmed hearts create the hollyhock below.

CENTER–Small and medium sun layered.

LEAVES–Large and small maple leaves snipped with deckle scissors and placed randomly to create a hollyhock stalk.

It's easy to simulate floral designs found on keepsake invitations, cards and photographs with a little punch creativity.

Home Tweet Home
MARILYN GARNER

BIRDHOUSE & VINE–Large house, ¼" round hand punch, heart hand punch and hand-cut poles.

BIRDHOUSE ROOF–Large house. Cut portion of large house out of black paper to form roof.

FLOWERS AND BUTTERFLY–Small tulip, mini flower and ⅛" round hand punch. Mini butterfly is folded for 3-dimensional affect.

WEATHER VANE–Portion of large snowflake for arrow, small rabbit, hand-cut post.

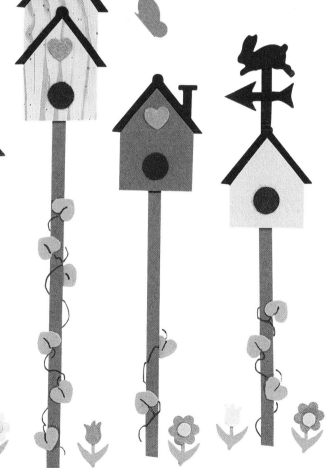

Garden Stakes
ERICA PIEROVICH

Stakes are hand-cut strips with rounded tops placed above offset punched medium circles (see page 7).

TAGS–Medium rectangle.
TOMATO–⁵⁄₁₆" round hand punch, star hand punch.
LETTUCE–Hand-cut design.
STRAWBERRY–Mini heart, mini sun.
CARROT–Small carrot punch.
CUCUMBER–Portion of foot punch.
TULIP–Mini tulip.
SQUASH–Mini apple, mini maple leaf.
RADISH–Mini heart, holly leaf.

Summer Basket
ERICA PIEROVICH

Mini square, mini apple, mini maple leaf, ⁵⁄₁₆" round hand punch, star hand punch, small tulip.

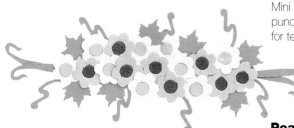

Basket Full of Posies
KATHLEEN PANEITZ

BASKET–Mini square, negative pieces from hearts and flowers border for handle and lower trim.

FLOWERS–Mini flower, ⅛" round hand punch.

LEAVES–Mini maple leaf, negative pieces from scroll border for tendrils.

Posy Bough
KATHLEEN PANEITZ

Mini flower, mini maple leaf, ⅛" round hand punch, negative pieces from scroll border for tendrils.

Pea Pods
ERICA PIEROVICH

Large moon, medium spiral, small strawberry, ¼" round hand punch. Pod seam is offset punched from large moon on dark green paper. Pod tip is a portion of large moon layered.

Butterfly and Bumble Bee Border
TONYA JEPPSON

BUTTERFLY BODY–Trimmed negative pieces from heart frame.
HEAD–Tear drop extension. Hand-draw antennae.
WINGS–Small oval, accented with negative pieces from tear drop decorative corner.

BUMBLE BEE BODY–Small egg.
HEAD–Small oval.
STINGER–Tear drop hand punch.
STRIPES–Hand-cut.
WINGS–Hand draw.

Annual

MARILYN GARNER

Here's a happy union between a garden planted with children and a garden planted with flowers and produce.

Dianthus Annual

Small triangle trimmed with deckle scissors, star hand punch.

Sunflower

Small egg, small sun, ¼" round hand punch.

Black-Eyed Nathan

Small sun, small egg, large birch leaf.

Garden Pages
MARILYN GARNER

Watermelon, carrots, large strawberry, sun, pumpkins and eggplant on seed packets are hand-cut.

WATERMELON—Watermelon on ground is offset punched from large circle with medium hearts for leaves.

CARROTS—Carrots on ground are small egg tucked behind brown paper "dirt" with large oak leaf tops.

STRAWBERRY—Strawberries on ground are small egg accented with small sun.

SUNFLOWER—Medium sun, small circle, small egg for leaves.

PUMPKIN—Medium and small hearts for leaves. Hand-cut pumpkins.

EGGPLANT—Hand-cut; small egg for leaves.

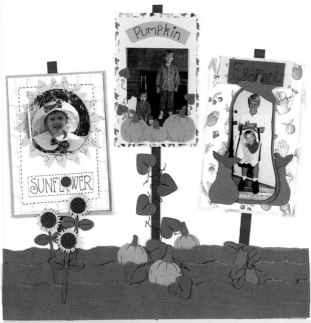

Tulips and Squares Border
ERICA PIEROVICH

Small square, mini square, small tulip.

Posies and Squares Border
ERICA PIEROVICH

Mini square, mini flower, ¼" round
hand punch.

Spiral Blossom Border
DEBBIE HUTCHINGS

Small circle, small spiral, small strawberry,
mini square.

Pansies All Around Frame
PAM METZGER, PHOTO DEBBIE HEWITT

Large birch leaf, medium apple, small apple,
small heart, ⅛" round hand punch
(see page 9 for layering technique).

seaside

Florida Coastline Page
ERICA PIEROVICH
PHOTOS COURTESY WENDY MCKEEHAN

FISH–Layer old tree with two large moons as shown. Add small fish (head), medium moons (smaller fins), and mini heart for lips. Embellish body with mini hearts, add eye of ⅛" and ¹⁄₁₆" round hand punches.

SEA URCHIN–Large sun cut.

SAND DOLLAR–Large circle, negative pieces from tear drop corner lace punch. Snip into large circle edges with ¹⁄₁₆" round hand punch.

Castles Under the Sea
KATHLEEN PANEITZ

Small castle, medium rectangle, small square, square hand punch, small turtle, small crab, small scorpion, ¹⁄₁₆" round hand punch.

Coral Reef
ERICA PIEROVICH

STARFISH–Medium star, portions of large sun, diamond extension.

SEAWEED–Negative pieces from hearts and flowers border.

CLAM–Small shell, ¹⁄₁₆" round hand punch.

SEA URCHIN–Large sun cut.

Tropical Sun Border
PAM METZGER

Large sun, small pineapple, small palm tree. Draw line with a wavy ruler.

camping

Wilderness Border
MARYJO REGIER

Top to bottom: medium rectangle, medium tree, small tree, negative pieces from tree decorative corner, diamond mini extension, large reindeer, small oak leaf, small maple leaf, mini sun/moon, star hand punch, small triangle, rectangle hand punch (for tent door), small dove (trimmed to make fish), negative piece of hearts and flowers border.

Boot Track Border
PAM METZGER

Mini diamond extension, negative pieces from hearts and flowers border, negative pieces from filmstrip border.

Campsite
JOANN COLLEDGE

Large tree, small horse.

MOUNTAINS–Large heart inverted and trimmed, medium sun.

TENTS–Top of large house with chimney removed.

CAMPFIRE–Large sun, hand-cut logs.

Campfire
ERICA PIEROVICH

Medium rectangle halved, small maple leaf.

Ashton at Lake Tahoe Page
NIKKI PATRICK

Small cloud, tear drop extension, large tree trimmed.

Ashton·Lake·Tahoe·August 1997

fourth of july

Apples Americana
NARDA POE

Large apple, small circle, small star.
Hand-cut 1½" squares.

Watermelon Hearts

Large heart, medium heart,
tear drop extension.

4th of July Page
KATHLEEN PANEITZ, PHOTOS LINDA HARRISION

Medium star, small star
(see page 7 for punch positioning),
mini star, negative pieces from hearts
and flowers border for streamers.

Streamin' Stars (right)
KATHLEEN PANEITZ

Medium rectangle, small star,
mini star, negative pieces from
hearts and flowers border. (See
page 7 for punch positioning.)

Patriotic Star Swag
ERICA PIEROVICH

Large star cut and layered.

Patriotic Fireworks (bottom right)
ERICA PIEROVICH

Medium rectangle, small spiral, negative
pieces from decorative star corner.

Balloon Streamers
AMANDA WILSON

Large balloon glued "sandwich" style to metallic streamers.

Vellum Package
PAM METZGER

Medium circle, medium heart halved.

BORDER—Offset punched medium circles (see page 7 for offset punching technique), ¼" round hand punch, mini hearts. Cover all surfaces with vellum paper for the soft look shown above.

Birthday Cake
AMANDA WILSON

LEAVES—Medium heart curled.

FLOWERS—Medium hearts halved and rolled around toothpick. Each flower has a layer of six, four, then three heart halves, each curled progressively tighter (see page 7 for adding dimension techniques).

TOP EDGING—Small heart folded and curled, oval hand punch.

BOTTOM EDGING—Medium heart folded and curled.

Celebrate! Gift Card
NIKKI PATRICK

Small snowflake, large sun, large bow, small bow. Boxes are hand-cut.

Pop-Up Bear Gift Tag
ERICA PIEROVICH

Medium bear, mini triangle, mini sun, bear corner punch (see Christmas Tree Pop-Up on page 44 for instructions).

Happy Birthday Banner
PAM KLASSEN

Use die cut letters for base and decorate with punched shapes. Left to right: small cake, mini sun, small triangle, small circle, ⅛" round hand punch, small egg, small oval, star hand punch, silhouette bow, oval hand punch, small cloud, small candy, tear drop extension, small star, mini star, small balloon, medium rectangle halved, small bow, entire negative piece of ribbon border, small sun.

Birthday celebrations are brimming with balloons, cake, ice cream, and presents. And you can re-create the whole party with punch art!

Pirate Party Birthday Page
KATHLEEN PANEITZ/MARYJO REGIER

SHIP–Large circle offset punched (see page 7 for technique) for sails, large circle halved for boat, small bone, small triangle, mini triangle, negative pieces of hearts and flowers border for waves. Hand-cut mast.

PIRATE BALLOONS–Large balloon layered, small triangle. Hand-draw faces.

TREASURE CHEST–Three large circle halves layered for top, medium rectangle, small fleur-de-lis, ¼" round hand punch, ⅛" round hand punch. Metallic paper used for coins.

SHIP WHEEL & SEA CREATURES– Large circle, medium circle, medium rectangle cut for center spokes, tear drop extension, ¼" round hand punch. Small scorpion, small crab, small turtle.

Birthday Train Border
ERICA PIEROVICH

TRACKS–Small cross.

TRAIN–Left to right: small cloud, small train engine, ¼" round hand punch, ⅛" round hand punch, medium rectangle, medium scallop, rectangle hand punch.

ANIMALS–Small seal, small lion, small rhino, small elephant.

western

Yipee-Yi-O! Cowboys, lassos, guitars and spurs.
Images of the wild and not-so-wild west abound.

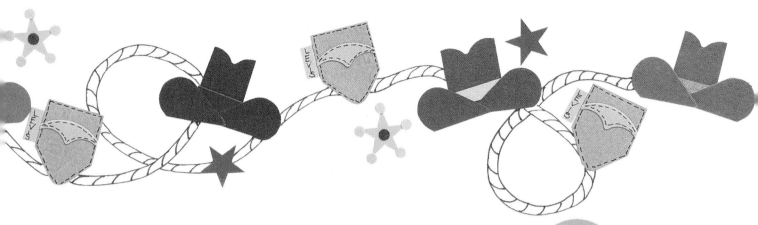

Western Border
PAM KLASSEN/ERICA PIEROVICH

Hand-draw rope.

BADGE/STAR–Small star, ⅛" round hand punch.
POCKET–Large heart, negative piece from heart frame.
HAT–Medium heart.

Hand-cut pocket tag and hat band. Embellish with pen stroking. (See steps right.)

A large heart, portion from heart frame and hand-cut tag combine to become a pocket.

A medium heart and hand-cut band are transformed into a ten-gallon hat.

Roadrunner
PAM KLASSEN

BODY–Old tree with top and trunk trimmed.
WING–Large birch leaf trimmed.
TAIL–Half large tree without trunk.
HEAD & BEAK–Large tree trimmed.
LEGS & FEET–Hand-cut legs, mini moons.

A large circle and large heart are hand cut for the body. Add trimmed medium rectangles and small square for the neck. Tunefully arrange small circle and ⅛" round hand punch.

Cowboy Tim Page
PAM METZGER

ROPE–Small ovals with the ends trimmed.

LARGE STAR–Small triangles and small spiral.

PEPPER–Portion of large sun trimmed and top of small strawberry.

BOOT–Trimmed rectangles, small star, small sun and ¼" round hand punch.

FENCE–Trimmed medium rectangle.

GUITAR–Large circle, large heart, medium rectangle, small circle, small square, ⅛" round hand punch. Hand-draw strings (see steps on previous page).

Feathers
MARILYN GARNER

Large birch leaf. Snip one leaf at top to form feather tip; layer with second leaf of complementary color. Snip edges. Embellish with pen stroking.

Horse Stampede
JOYCE FEIL

Medium horse, small spiral.

Cactus Pot Border
MARYJO REGIER

Southwest border encircling container, portion of large snowflake, mini sun layered.

Southwest Border
PAM KLASSEN

Medium diamond, diamond hand punch, 1⁄16" round hand punch (see page 8 for punch guideline techniques).

The Southwest sizzles with sunshine, coyote and cactus.
Capture the mood with these desert borders.

Canyon Road Page (opposite page)
DEBBIE HUTCHINGS

TOP BORDER–Small cross, negative piece from southwest border #1. Punch one row of crosses. Punch a second row of opposing crosses (see detail at right). With ruler and craft knife, cut away bottom portion from each row of crosses. Add negative piece from southwest border #1 as an embellishment.

MATS FOR LETTERING–Top portion of small cross punched at an angle across top and bottom of rectangular paper mat.

BOTTOM BORDER–Small cross. Layer two strips of alternating punched crosses as explained in top border.

Howling Coyote Border
ERICA PIEROVICH

Small coyote, medium spiral.

Arizona Border (below)
DEBBIE HUTCHINGS

Small triangle. Punch one row of triangles. Punch a second row of triangles matching triangle bases together. With ruler and craft knife, cut away top portions from each row of triangles to achieve final border. (See page 8 for punch guidelines for achieving accuracy on punched borders.)

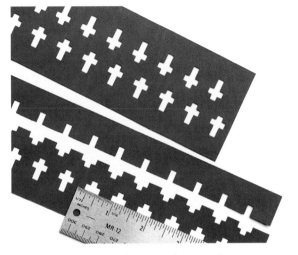

When trimmed, rows of crosses form a unique southwestern border.

Desert Animal Border (right)
MARYJO REGIER

Top to bottom: medium horse, small diamond, diamond mini extension, portion of medium snowflake, mini sun, medium spiral, triangle hand punch, large bear, 1/16" round hand punch, large circle, small coyote. Horse and bear are layered from behind with orange paper after being punched with hand punches.

decorative dutch art

Dutch art lends itself beautifully to the magic of punches and the creative use of color.

Dutch Art Frames
PAM METZGER, BOTTOM PHOTO DAVID URE

Large heart, small heart, small oval, tear drop hand punch, medium tulip, mini flower, ⅛" round hand punch. Hand-cut stems. Small hearts halved for smallest leaves, heart embellishments. Tulip steps are shown below. (See page 9 for another example of how paper choices can affect the outcome of your design.)

Amanda Page
PAM METZGER/PAM KLASSEN
PHOTO PORTRAITS PLUS

Hand-cut stems are embellished with small spiral. Accent with tear drop extension, negative pieces from scallop border and hearts and flowers border, ⅛" round hand punch.

HEART ENDS–Large heart, medium heart, small heart, mini flower, ¼" round hand punch. Large purple heart halved and layered with large blue heart, then medium green heart. Center motif is small purple heart halved, dark pink mini flower, blue ¼" round hand punch.

TULIPS–Medium tulip, mini heart. Teal, purple, magenta medium tulip trimmed; pink mini heart.

CORNER FLOWERS–Large scallop, large heart, medium heart, small heart, mini flower, ⁵⁄₁₆" round hand punch. Portions of green and purple large scallops layered; large blue heart halved layered with medium pink heart halved; small green heart, mini blue flower; blue ⁵⁄₁₆" round.

TEAR DROP ENDS–Medium heart, small heart, mini heart, small circle, tear drop extension, ⁵⁄₁₆" round hand punch. Magenta ⁵⁄₁₆" round; medium green heart halved and layered with blue ⁵⁄₁₆" round, small green heart halved and pink mini heart halved; purple ⁵⁄₁₆" round on top.

Two shades of blue give the punched shapes in the above Dutch art frame its cool, monochromatic feel...

...while deep red, black, burnt umber and goldenrod lend this frame a timeless, classic touch...

Layering and cutting with different colored papers adds dimension and diversity to punch art.

...and bright, primary hues command a sense of elementary fun!

victorian

Re-create the romance of the Victorian era with punch art lace, ribbons and flowers.

Calin and Skylar Page
AMY TALARICO, PHOTO DAVID URE

Large heart, mini heart, 1/16" round hand punch. Punch mini heart and 1/16" round hand punch out of large heart as shown. Layer two colors of large hearts for alternating affect. Group layered hearts to create lacy edge.

Pattie with Doll Page
MARILYN GARNER

Small circle, small spiral, small egg, medium heart, small tulip. Heart frame is hand cut.

Calin Rose and Skylar Blue

Pattie with doll Marietta, ga 1948

Tea Party Picture Frame
AMY TALARICO, PHOTO JOYCE FEIL

INNER FRAME–Rectangle hand punch, silhouette bow, $1/16$" round hand punch. Hand-cut paper strips 1" wide; trim both sides with scallop scissors. Punch $1/16$" rounds around frame. Rectangle hand punch holes at intervals; weave hand-cut strips of purple paper through holes.

MIDDLE FRAME–Tear drop corner lace edge, $1/16$" round hand punch. Hand-cut $6½ \times 5$" pale pink frame. Punch as shown; trim with scallop scissors and mount on slightly larger dark purple mat.

OUTER FRAME–Mini flower, $1/8$" round hand punch, small bow. Hand-cut $7½ \times 6$" lavendar mat with large scallop scissors. Punch mini flowers; add dark pink $1/8$" rounds to flower centers. Place small bow and $1/8$" rounds at each corner; mount to larger white mat trimmed with scallop scissors. Mount to second white mat trimmed with scallop scissors and punched with $1/8$" round hand punch.

Tea Party Invitation
JOYCE FEIL

CURTAINS–Small bow, $1/8$" round hand punch, $1/16$" round hand punch, negative pieces from scroll border. Curtain is edged with scallop scissors.

TEAPOT–Christmas ornament cut, portion of large bow, negative pieces from scroll border, small spiral.

CUPS–Christmas ornament cut, negative pieces from scroll border for steam.

TABLECLOTH–Tear drop corner lace, negative pieces from scroll border, $1/16$" round hand punch. Tablecloths are hand cut; white tablecloth is edged using scallop scissors.

PLACE MATS–Large scallop cut, mini flower, $1/8$" round hand punch, mini birch leaf.

TABLE LEGS–Portion of large rubber stamp.

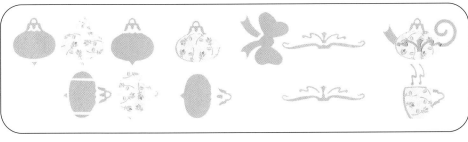

By adding pieces from a bow, a scroll border and spiral, an ornament becomes an elegant teapot. Turn the same ornament on its side to make a tea cup.

Heart of Hearts
ERICA PIEROVICH

Small heart, mini heart, negative pieces from hearts and flowers border. Here's a good use of the offset punching technique shown on page 7.

Chloe
Jan 18, 1998

Winter coat and hat made
with love by Grammy

Tear Drop Wreath
PAM METZGER

Tear drop extension, negative pieces from hearts and flowers border.

Chloe Page
JOANN COLLEDGE

Small maple leaf, ⅛" round hand punch, negative pieces from heart frame.

Leaf and Berry Wreath
ERICA PIEROVICH

Large maple leaf, small maple leaf, mini maple leaf, ¼" round hand punch, silhouette bow.

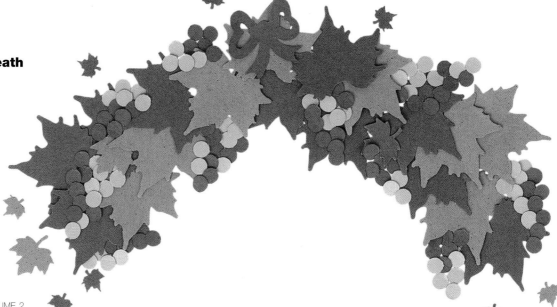

A small flower bud is made by snipping a small egg with a mini sun and layering it over another small egg then layering it on top with a medium tulip.

Portions of a small snowflake layered over a small bell, then layered with medium tulip to make a bell flower.

A large flower bud is created by layering three small strawberries over a small egg.

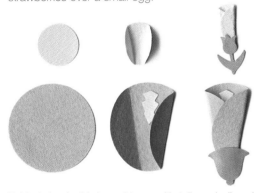

Fold circles in thirds and layer with tulip or bell and portion of snowflake to create tubular flowers.

Margaret and Pattie Page
MARILYN GARNER

PINK ON PINK MOTIFS–Large birch leaf, small bell, small tulip.
CORNER BELLS–Small bell, medium tulip, portions of small snowflake cut.
TOP FLORAL SWAG–Small bell, small strawberry, medium daisy, small sun.
BOTTOM FLORAL SWAG–Small bell, medium tulip, portions of small snowflake, large birch leaf, large circle folded in thirds, portions of large snowflake, large tulip, small circle folded in thirds, small egg offset punched with small sun, large daisy, large sun, small snowflake.

Fleur-de-Lis Border
DEBBIE HUTCHINGS

Arrange four small fleur-de-lis shapes to create each flower and connect flowers to make border (see page 9 for more on combining shapes).

Walk through our winter wonderland of punch art!
From greeting cards to luminarias,
there's no end to what your punches can do.

Window of Snowflakes
PAM KLASSEN

Use any combination of punches on hand to make your own unique snowflakes like those at left. These snowflakes are first hand cut from vellum paper and then embellished with white punched shapes.

Frosty's Page
CONNIE DOYLE

Cut 1½" strips of paper. Cut strips into lengths varying from 1" to 9" with a variety of decorative scissors.

TOP BORDER–Scroll border, large bell, small star, star decorative corner, heart hand punch, small angel, large heart, medium heart, small snowflake.

BOTTOM BORDER–Small star, small snowflake, small tree, small heart.

SIDE BORDERS–Top to bottom: negative pieces from fleur-de-lis frame, small cross, mini flower, tear drop hand punch, large snowflake, small heart, small dove, medium heart, scroll border, star decorative corner, small star, large tree, small tree.

CENTER–Small star, medium heart, small snowflake, small heart, negative piece from star decorative corner, tear drop hand punch. Trim outer edge of heart and photo mat with mini scallop scissors.

Snowflake Wedding Page

PAM KLASSEN, PHOTO DAVID A. ZISER

These delicate flakes are made by combining several different punched shapes. They employ the technique of removing guides from corner punches, described on page 7.

SNOWFLAKE 1–Snowflake frame is negative pieces from lace clover decorative corner. ⅛" round hand punch. Negative pieces from: celestial border (see celestial border on envelope, page 37), southwest border #2, scallop decorative corner and tear drop corner lace edge.

SNOWFLAKE 2–Snowflake frame is negative pieces from Victorian decorative corner. Diamond hand punch, ⅛" round hand punch. Negative pieces from: celestial border, southwest border #2 and diamond decorative corner.

SNOWFLAKE 3–Snowflake frame is negative pieces from corner lace. Mini moon hand punch, mini fleur-de-lis, triangle hand punch.

SNOWFLAKE 4–Snowflake frame is negative pieces from mini scallop corner lace. Diamond hand punch. Negative pieces from: country hearts border and southwest border #2.

Snowflake Pattern

DEBBIE HUTCHINGS

Create a snowflake pattern by combining six large snowflakes in a circle and embellishing with tear drop extension as shown above right.

A cut large circle combined with pieces of Santa, large and mini moon, mini oak leaf, and ¼" round hand punch becomes a blue jay.

Blue Jay on Pine Bough
PAM KLASSEN

PINE CONES—Hand-cut pine cones with scallop scissors. Moon hand punch, portions of large sun.

BLUE JAY—Large circle, small Santa, large moon, mini moon, mini oak leaf, ¼" round hand punch.

Cat in Window
PAM KLASSEN

Small square, small cat. Hand-cut 1" x 1½" brown rectangle. Punch six squares from snowflake paper and glue to brown rectangle to form window frame. Hand-cut window sill, add small cat.

Stained Glass Frame
NIKKI PATRICK, PHOTO PARTY CRASHERS PHOTOGRAPHY

Place randomly cut colored paper around photo. Cover with three rows of southwestern #2 border punched and trimmed from black paper.

Snow Globe
PAM KLASSEN

Diamond mini extension, ⅛" round hand punch, large tree, silhouette cottage, large house, portion of small castle (church spire), mini square, rectangle hand punch, negative piece from scroll border (chimney smoke). Use a 6¼" circle template on blue and white paper to create globe and snow drifts. Hand-cut base. Make snow for roofs by punching and cutting portion of house and cottage out of white paper.

Add Christmas charm to a large tree by punching with a ¹⁄₁₆" round hand punch, cutting with deckle scissors, and layering over a gold large tree.

Line of Mittens Border
PAM METZGER

MITTENS—Large balloon, small egg for thumbs and cut rectangle for cuffs.

MITTEN DECORATIONS—Left to right:
1 SNOWFLAKE—Small snowflake, negative pieces from hearts and flowers border, negative pieces from film strip border.
2 ARGYLE—Mini diamond.
3 HEART—Negative pieces from hearts and flowers border, small heart.
4 SNOWFLAKE—Medium snowflake, negative pieces from hearts and flowers border.
5 FLOWER—Mini flower, ⅛" round hand punch, negative pieces from hearts and flowers border.
6 CHECKERBOARD—Mini square, negative pieces from country hearts border.

CLOTHESPINS—Petals from medium daisy, ⅛" round hand punch.

Rocky Mountain Winter Fun Page
ERICA PIEROVICH

Large tree punched and layered, negative pieces from snowflake decorative corner, small square, ⅛" and ¹⁄₁₆" round hand punches.

Snowman Border
PAM KLASSEN

BODY—Large heart, large circle, small circle for arms and head.
HAT—Medium star cut.
SCARF—Large bow cut.
SHOVEL—Medium tulip, hand-cut handle.
BUTTONS—⅛" round hand punch.
EYES—¹⁄₁₆" round hand punch.

Luminarias
NIKKI PATRICK

Use a variety of punches to make ordinary gift bags extraordinary lanterns. Punch while the bag is folded flat for symmetry. Star decorative corner, diamond mini extension, large snowflake used on luminarias at left.

Card and Envelope
MARYJO REGIER

CARD–Corner lace clover.
SNOWMAN–Large circle, medium circle, small circle, negative pieces from scroll border for arms. Hand-draw eyes and mouth. Tear drop extension for nose.
SWAG–Small star, small house, small heart.
SKY/ENVELOPE EMBELLISHMENTS–Celestial border, star hand punch.

Pine Cone and Berries Frame
PAM METZGER, PHOTO JOYCE FEIL

A portion of a small maple leaf combines with a small triangle and medium rectangle to become a pine cone. Berries are small circles, ⅛" round hand punch.

Chloe's First Day of Winter Play Page
JOANN COLLEDGE

PHOTO/MAT–Small snowflake. Punch snowflake halfway into photo's edges. Add one-half of a white snowflake on black mat to complete design.

GREEN BACKGROUND–Stamp green paper with pine frond stamp. Use a craft knife to cut random slits into fronds and slip white punched snowflakes into slits.

christmas

The holidays are full of creative punch opportunities whether you are decorating or preserving memories.

Madeline's Christmas Page
JOANN COLLEDGE, PHOTO ELIZABETH WALLIS

Large holly, small spiral, ⁵⁄₁₆" round hand punch, ¼" round hand punch. Trim around some of the punch art and background paper to create a slit and insert photo to achieve overlay effect.

Christmas 1997

Madeline Wallis

"my princess dress"

Small Christmas Cards
JOANN COLLEDGE/MARILYN GARNER

ANGEL–Large heart, large circle, medium circle, small circle, ⅛" round hand punch, ¹⁄₁₆" round hand punch.

JOY WREATH–Angel frame, portions of large holly, ⅛" round hand punch.

NOEL BASKET–Corner lace, small square cut in half, large circle, medium circle, large holly, ⅛" round hand punch.

Christmas Tree Card
MARILYN GARNER

Hand-cut base, tree trunk and branches. Hand-draw faces and embellishments.

ANGEL–¼" round hand punch, small egg, small heart (arms), large birch leaf cut (wings).
HOLLY–⅛" round hand punch, large holly.
REINDEER–Top portion of small bow (reindeer ears), small egg.
APPLE–Small apple.
WREATH–¼" round hand punch, small circle.
HEART & BELL–Small heart, mini heart, small bell.
JINGLE BELL–Small circle.
STAR–Small star, star hand punch.
GINGERBREAD MAN–Small bear trimmed.
SNOWMAN–Large bow (trimmed for snowman's jacket), small circle, ¼" round hand punch.
STAR & TREE–Star hand punch, small tree.

House & Tree Border
NARDA POE

Large house, large tree, small circle, ⅛" round hand punch.

Snowmen Border
PAM METZGER

Medium circle, small circle, ¼" round hand punch, ⅛" round hand punch, rectangle trimmed with fancy scissors for scarf.

Holly & Present Border
NARDA POE

Large holly, ¼" round hand punch, hand-cut strip, medium heart halved with tear drop extension punched out.

On all three borders, hand-cut background squares. Embellish borders with pen stroke stitching.

All Star Santa Border
PAM METZGER

BODY–Large star, mini triangle.
HEAD/BEARD–Small circle, small cloud, small triangle, ⅛" round hand punch, ¹⁄₁₆" round hand punch, hand-cut mouth.
BELT–Mini square, hand-cut strip with tiny square from southwest border for belt.

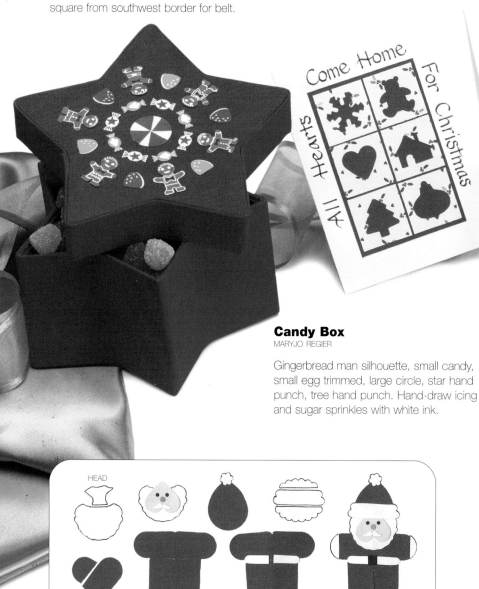

Candy Box
MARYJO REGIER

Gingerbread man silhouette, small candy, small egg trimmed, large circle, star hand punch, tree hand punch. Hand-draw icing and sugar sprinkles with white ink.

All Hearts Come Home for Christmas Card
PAM KLASSEN

Medium punches: Snowflake, bear, heart, house, tree, Christmas ornament.

May Your Holidays Be Bright Christmas Card
PAM KLASSEN

Mini and small oval. Punch mini ovals in card, mount small ovals in various colors behind cutouts. Hand draw-string.

Ho Ho Ho Santa Card
DEBBIE HUTCHINGS

Punch, cut and assemble Santa as shown at left. Add small stars position punched with star hand punch. (See page 7 for punch positioning technique.)

SANTA HEAD–Old tree trimmed, medium heart, large balloon, mini flower, portion of large scallop, ⅛" round hand punch, ¹⁄₁₆" round hand punch, tear drop hand punch for moustache.

BODY–Large heart trimmed, portion of large scallop with mini square for belt.

Christmas Candelabra
NIKKI PATRICK

Large holly, rectangle, mini star, small egg, small lips, ⅛" round hand punch. Poinsettias and candle flames are cut from lips.

Toy Soldier
ERICA PIEROVICH

HEAD—Large bell, medium heart, small heart (top of hat), small tulip, mini sun, small angel wing on hat, hand-cut band.

BODY—Large bell, large heart, small heart, mini moon, ⅛" round hand punch. Belt is hand cut. Embellish sleeves and buckle with negative pieces from scroll border.

LEGS—Medium rectangle, medium heart, large bell. Embellish cuffs and pockets with negative pieces from scroll border.

STAFF—Hand-cut staff, small fleur-de-lis.

Heart Trees
DEBBIE HUTCHINGS

Small heart, medium heart, large heart, rectangle trimmed.

Christmas Tree Border
ERICA PIEROVICH

Large tree, diamond mini extension.

Tree of Hearts Page
MARILYN GARNER

Large heart, medium heart, small heart, medium star, small star, heart hand punch, rectangle.

Holly Leaf Christmas Tree
ERICA PIEROVICH

Large holly, medium rectangle, medium star, diamond mini extension.

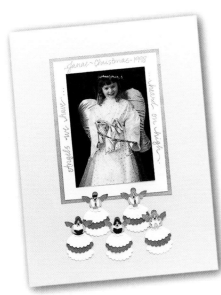

Lacy Angel Page
EILEEN RUSCETTA, PHOTO KATHLEEN PANEITZ

SKIRT–Large scallop trimmed in graduating layers.
BODICE–Small butterfly.
WINGS/ARMS–Small lip trimmed.
FACE/HAIR/HALO–¼" round hand punch, portions of small snowflake cut, ¹⁄₁₆" round hand punch.
OTHER–Portion of snowflake for garland; hand-cut candle, flame and hands; negative pieces from diamond decorative corner for song book.

Diamond Border
KATHLEEN PANEITZ

Small diamond, negative piece from scroll border, ⅛" round hand punch.

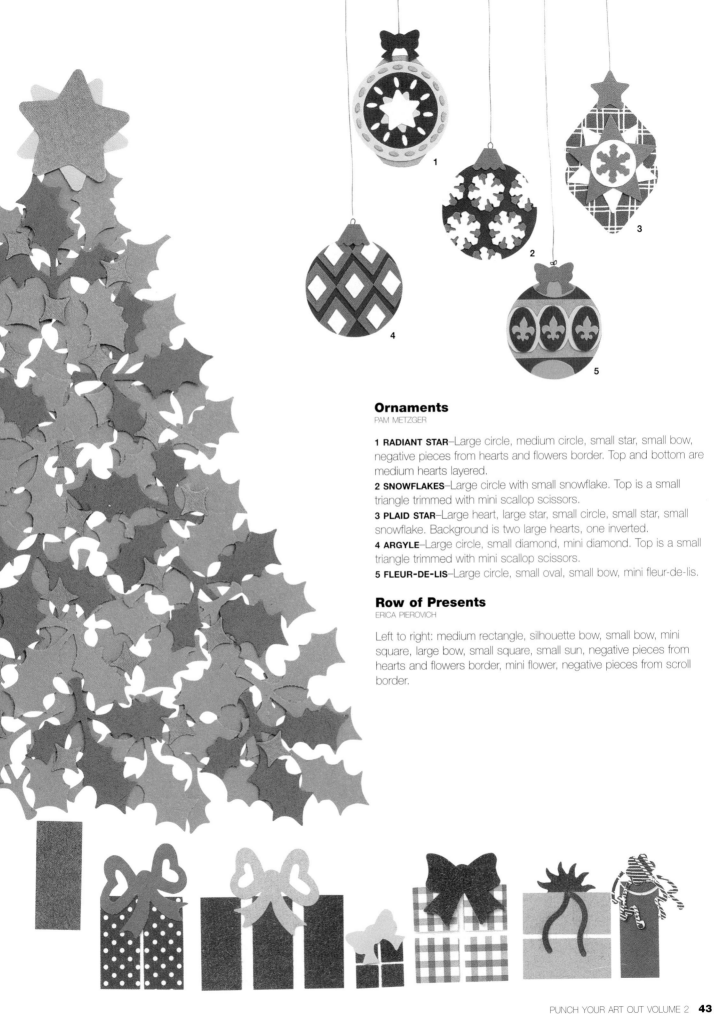

Ornaments
PAM METZGER

1 RADIANT STAR–Large circle, medium circle, small star, small bow, negative pieces from hearts and flowers border. Top and bottom are medium hearts layered.

2 SNOWFLAKES–Large circle with small snowflake. Top is a small triangle trimmed with mini scallop scissors.

3 PLAID STAR–Large heart, large star, small circle, small star, small snowflake. Background is two large hearts, one inverted.

4 ARGYLE–Large circle, small diamond, mini diamond. Top is a small triangle trimmed with mini scallop scissors.

5 FLEUR-DE-LIS–Large circle, small oval, small bow, mini fleur-de-lis.

Row of Presents
ERICA PIEROVICH

Left to right: medium rectangle, silhouette bow, small bow, mini square, large bow, small square, small sun, negative pieces from hearts and flowers border, mini flower, negative pieces from scroll border.

1 Angel Face
MARILYN GARNER

Large birch leaf trimmed, medium heart inverted, small egg, corner rounder. Hand-draw face, halo and lettering.

2 Holly Ornament
DEBBIE HUTCHINGS

Large holly, silhouette ornament.

3 Winnie the Pooh's Let It Snow
DEBBIE HUTCHINGS

OUTSIDE—100 Acre Pooh Smiles frame backed with black paper, small snowflake, hand-drawn pen stroke stitching and lettering.

INSIDE—Large tree, small snowflake, small 100 Acre Pooh, small 100 Acre Tigger.

POP-UP—Fold white base paper in half and keep closed. With straight scissors cut three ½" parallel strips into the fold. Open base paper and bend strips out. Glue tree, Pooh and Tigger to front half of strips.

4 Ho Ho Ho Reindeer
MARILYN GARNER

Small egg, bottom portion of small bow trimmed, ⅛" round hand punch. Hand-draw antlers, face and lettering.

5 Tree and Snowflakes
ERICA PIEROVICH

Tree double frame, large circle for background, star hand punch, negative pieces from snowflake decorative corner, corner rounder, corner lace rounder.

6 Flying Angel
MARILYN GARNER

Small heart inverted, medium heart, small egg, ⁵⁄₁₆" round hand punch. Hand-draw halo, face and lettering.

7 Christmas Tree Pop-Up
ERICA PIEROVICH

Medium tree, star hand punch, corner lace rounder.

POP-UP—Fold green base paper in half and keep closed. Punch medium tree ½" in from fold. Set aside the positive punched tree shapes. Hand-cut two strips of brown paper ¼" wide by ½" long. Open green base paper and slide half of brown strip to outside of base paper at tree trunk and attach. Attach other half to base of tree trunk on positive punched tree shapes. Place stars on top of trees and glue stars together.

hanukkah

Happy Hanukkah Page

ERICA PIEROVICH/EILEEN RUSCETTA
PHOTO KIM TRACHTMAN

FRAME—Mini sun. Glue sun half-way under mat as shown.

MENORAH BASE—Negative pieces from scroll border, portion of rubber stamp trimmed.

CANDLES—Small circle, mini sun, negative pieces from tear drop corner lace for flames. Candle sticks are hand cut.

STAR OF DAVID—Small triangle, mini triangle.

DREIDELS—Small dreidel layered, small spiral. Hand-draw Hebrew characters in gold ink.

Holly Border

MARILYN GARNER

Large holly, star hand punch. Draw line with wavy ruler.

Additional instructions

Below are instructions for additional projects shown throughout the book.

PAM METZGER

Inside Cover Art

HEART—Large heart, medium heart, small heart, mini flower, ¼" round hand punch. Large pink polka-dot heart halved and layered with large purple heart, then medium green heart. Center motif is small yellow polka-dot heart halved, pink mini flower, purple ⅛" round hand punch.

TULIP—Medium tulip layered and cut, ⅛" round hand punch. Tulip on inside cover is layered with green, purple, pink and yellow polka-dot papers. Yellow and green ⅛" rounds for accents. (See page 27 for tulip details).

Title Page Art

FLOWERS—Clockwise from center top: layer 3 medium scallops and small circle, add 2 large birch leaves, accent with ⅛" round hand punch; arrange 2½" large hearts and decorate with portions of hearts and flowers border, ⅛" round hand punch, small egg, mini tear drops, small circle cut in half; layer 2 medium tulips and accent with negative pieces from scallop border; cut large circle with fancy scissors, layer with 2 medium daisies, medium circle, small circle, 2 large birch leaves; layer 2 cut medium daisies with small oval and small heart; 3 half hearts, cut medium apple, 3 mini tear drops.

HEART—Large heart, medium heart, ⅛" round hand punch.

LEAVES/STEMS—Negative pieces from hearts and flowers border, medium scallop, small spiral, large birch leaf trimmed and folded, mini birch leaf, negative pieces from scroll border.

Picket Fence (Contents page)

Small cross, small sun halved, mini maple leaf, negative pieces from scroll border, and scallop border, ⅛" round hand punch.

Party in a Box (page 3)

Medium rectangle, ⅛" round hand punch, small bow, small balloon, small heart, small star, star hand punch, negative pieces from hearts and flowers border.

Summer Wreath
(page 3)

Hand-cut thin, 2" circle for base.
FLOWERS—Mini flower, ⅛" round hand punch, small spiral.
WATERMELON—Large circle offset punched, ¹⁄₁₆" round hand punch.
PEAR—Portion of rubber stamp handle.
APPLES—Small apple, top of small strawberry.
GRAPES—⅛" round hand punch, mini maple leaf.
PEACHES—⁵⁄₁₆" round hand punch, oval hand punch, hand-cut peach stems.

BUTTERFLY—Butterfly silhouette.
LEAVES/TENDRILS—Small maple leaf, negative pieces of scroll border.

Circle Dutch Art (above)

From back to front: Small oval, large heart, ¼" round hand punch, ⅛" round hand punch, large circle, small heart, small circle, circle extension, mini flower, mini heart, scallop scissors.

Bubble Tree (facing page)

Medium star, small circle, ⁵⁄₁₆" round hand punch, ¼" round hand punch, ⅛" round hand punch. Some circles are offset punched to achieve overlay affect. (See page 7 for offset punching technique.)

Christmas Wreath (facing page)

Hand-cut thin, 2" circle for base.
SNOWMAN—small circle, ⅛" round hand punch, hand-cut nose and hat.
MITTENS—small heart trimmed, small triangle layered, hand-cut mitten strings.
OTHER—Large holly cut, small snowflake, ¼" round hand punch, small star, star hand punch, small tree, small house.

Sources

Thanks to the following companies whose products are used in this book. Please check with your local retailers to find these materials.

PAM METZGER

Specialty Papers/Stamps

pages 10-11 Summer Lilacs
Paper Pizazz™ Pretty Papers, Hot Off The Press

page 12 Floral Design
Printable Papers™ MAB 8009, Frances Meyer

page 13 Hollyhock Accents
Paper Pizazz™ Pretty Papers, Hot Off The Press

page 13 Home Tweet Home
Natural pine paper #42-6106, Provo Craft

page 19 Apples Americana, Patriotic Star Swag, Patriotic Fireworks
White stars on navy and scarlet stripes, The Paper Patch

page 20 Happy Birthday Banner
Block alphabet, Ellison® Craft & Design
25862 Commercentre Dr., Lake Forest, CA 92630
1-800-253-2238, www.ellison.com

page 30 Chloe Page
Mayfair Imprintables card, George Stanley line, Mara-Mi (wholesale only)
650 Taft St. N.E., Minneapolis, MN 55413
1-800-627-2648

page 35 Cat in Window
White snowflakes on midnight blue paper, The Paper Patch

page 37 Chloe's First Day
Pine frond stamp, Stampin' Up!
6746 Hwy. 89
Kanab, UT 84741
1-800-STAMP UP

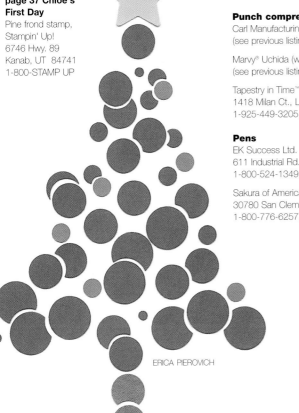

ERICA PIEROVICH

Punches/Scissors

All Night Media®, Inc. (wholesale only)
Box 10607, San Rafael, CA 94912
1-800-782-6733, www.allnightmedia.com

American Pin & Fastener (wholesale only)
PO Box 24238, Tempe, AZ 85285
1-602-968-6475

Carl Manufacturing of Hong Kong LTD. (wholesale only)
Rooms 1519-1520, Star House, 3 Salisbury Road
Tsimshatsui, Kowloon, Hong Kong
Tel. 852 2302 1488, www.venture-web.or.jp/carl

Family Treasures, Inc.
24922 Anza Ave. Unit A, Valencia, CA 91355-1229
1-800-413-2645, www.familytreasures.com

Fiskars®, Inc. (wholesale only)
7811 W. Stewart, Wausau, WI 54401
1-800-950-0203, www.fiskars.com

Marvy® Uchida (wholesale only)
3535 Del Amo Blvd., Torrance, CA 90503
1-800-541-5877, www.uchida.com

McGill, Inc. (wholesale only)
131 E. Prairie St., Marengo, IL 60152
1-800-982-9884

Nankong Enterprises, Inc. (wholesale only)
Polly Drummond Ctr., Suite 16E, Newark, DE 19711
1-302-731-2995, www.nankong.com

Punch compression aides

Carl Manufacturing of Hong Kong LTD. (see previous listing)

Marvy® Uchida (wholesale only) (see previous listing)

Tapestry in Time™
1418 Milan Ct., Livermore, CA 94550
1-925-449-3205, www.tapestryintime.com

Pens

EK Success Ltd. (wholesale only)
611 Industrial Rd., Carlstadt, NJ 07072
1-800-524-1349, www.eksuccess.com

Sakura of America (wholesale only)
30780 San Clemente St., Hayward, CA 94544-7131
1-800-776-6257, www.gellyroll.com

Adhesives

3M Stationery & Office Supplies Division
3M Center, St. Paul, MN 55144-1000
1-800-364-3577, www.3M.com

Tombow (Mono® Aqua) (wholesale only)
2000 Newpoint Place Pkwy., Lawrenceville, GA 30043
1-678-442-9224, www.tombowusa.com

The Gillette Company (DryLine® adhesive) (wholesale only)
Stationery Products Group, Prudential Tower Building,
Boston, MA 02199, 1-800-884-4443

Therm O Web (Sticky Dots and Therm O Web) (wholesale only)
770 Glenn Ave., Wheeling, IL 60090
1-847-520-5200, www.thermoweb.com

Xyron™ (wholesale only)
14698 No. 78th Wy., Scottsdale, AZ 85260
1-800-793-3523, www.xyron.com

Papers

Canson-Talens, Inc. (wholesale only)
21 Industrial Dr., South Hadley, MA 01075
1-800-628-9283, www.canson@aol.com

Creative Memories®
PO Box 1839, St. Cloud, MN 56302-1839
1-800-468-9335, www.creative-memories.com

Frances Meyer, Inc.® (wholesale only)
PO Box 3088, Savannah, GA 31402
1-912-748-5252, www.francesmeyer.com

Hot Off The Press (wholesale only)
1250 N.W. Third, Dept. B, Canby, OR 97013
1-503-266-9102, www.hotp.com

Northern Spy (wholesale only)
PO Box 2335, Placerville, CA 95667
1-530-620-7430, www.northernspy.com

The Paper Patch® (wholesale only)
PO Box 414, Riverton, UT 84065
1-801-253-3018

Paper Garden (wholesale only)
4224 Losee Rd., Suite F, No. Las Vegas, NV 89030
1-702-639-1900

Provo Craft (wholesale only)
285 E. 900 South, Provo, UT 84606
1-800-937-7686

Westrim Craft/Memories Forever (wholesale only)
9667 Canoga Ave., Chatsworth, CA 91311
1-800-727-2727, www.westrimcraft.com

Punch guide

The punch shapes below are some of the ones used most frequently throughout this book and are shown for your reference. Not all punches used in projects are shown below. Punch shapes are shown at 100% but may vary by manufacturer.

Large Punches

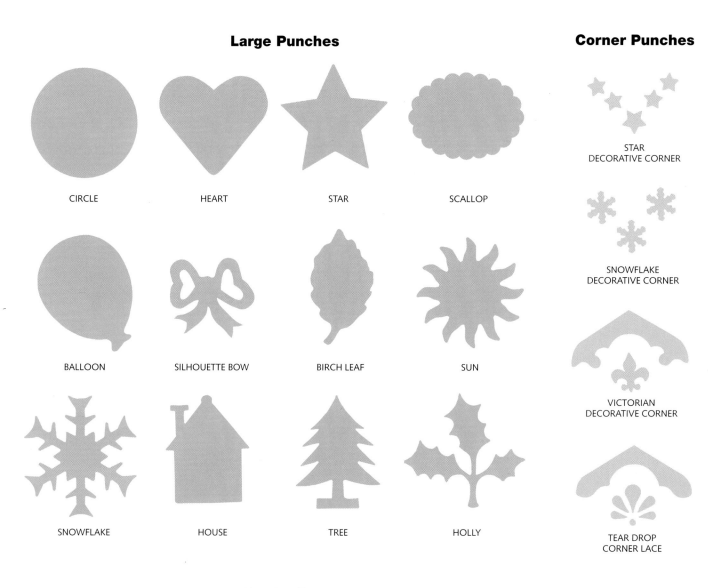

CIRCLE

HEART

STAR

SCALLOP

BALLOON

SILHOUETTE BOW

BIRCH LEAF

SUN

SNOWFLAKE

HOUSE

TREE

HOLLY

Corner Punches

STAR
DECORATIVE CORNER

SNOWFLAKE
DECORATIVE CORNER

VICTORIAN
DECORATIVE CORNER

TEAR DROP
CORNER LACE

Border Punches

SCALLOP

SOUTHWEST #1

SOUTHWEST #2

HEARTS AND FLOWERS

SCROLL

COUNTRY HEARTS